The Handbook for Exceptional People

G000144682

The Handbook for Exceptional People

Jez Cartwright

First published 2006 by Jez Cartwright

This edition published 2008 by Rodale
an imprint of Pan Macmillan Ltd
Pan Macmillan, 20 New Wharf Road, London N1 9RR
Basingstoke and Oxford
Associated companies throughout the world
www.panmacmillan.com

ISBN 978-1-9057-4412-1

9 8 7 6 5 4 3 2 1

A CIP catalogue record for this book is available from
the British Library.

Designed by James Cartledge
www.jamescartledge.co.uk

Printed and bound in Italy by Printer Trento

LIVE YOUR WHOLE LIFE™

We inspire and enable people to improve their lives and the world around them

Visit **www.panmacmillan.com** to read more about all our books
and to buy them. You will also find features, author interviews and
news of any author events, and you can sign up for e-newsletters
so that you're always first to hear about our new releases.

Contents

Introduction

Welcome to The Handbook for Exceptional People. You have picked up this book and started to read it for your own reasons. For some of you it will be because you liked the title or the colour of the cover, or perhaps a friend recommended it to you, or there may be any number of other reasons. Whatever they are you are obviously interested in the subject matter: Exceptional People.

I will start by saying that I believe everyone is exceptional. This includes you, the person who is sitting near to you and even the person who annoys you most of the time – they are exceptional, too.

The reality is, however, that most people are unaware of this. The reason for this is that the Exceptional Person is shrouded in layer upon layer of information and experiences from their past that whirrs around their brain, stopping them from being the Exceptional Person that lies at the core of who they really are.

Through my own personal journey, and the work that I do as a personal coach, I have seen many aspects of human behaviour. Some of the ways that we behave work well whereas others are less effective, and it is those ways that can create conflicts with other people or simply mean that we do not have the best relationships with them. This handbook is by no means intended to be a definitive text that will uncover the way that an Exceptional Person interacts and gets along with others, but rather as a guidebook to help you look at different areas of your life and to ask yourself questions about how past experiences might have affected how you deal with situations now.

Are the ways that you interact with others giving you what you want out of life? By asking yourself this and other similar questions you are opening up the possibility of an alternative way of living where you will be able to form stronger personal and business relationships, and will find getting on with others easier and more rewarding. By understanding yourself at a deep level you can see more clearly into the way you and others react to the challenges of life and even simple everyday situations. The result will be a clearer and purer way of communicating with others.

Just by reading this book you will become more consciously aware of your behaviour. You will find that some of the questions will appear time and time again. I make no apologies for this, as I believe that by asking these questions we will keep learning about ourselves, and the day we stop learning about ourselves will be the day we stop living.

Although many of you will choose to read the book in its entirety, others will dip into the sections that you see as relevant. I urge you at least to read it through once before using it as a reference tool. This will enable you to walk through the different parts of the book and build on your knowledge as you go along. If you carry out the exercises along the way you will be able to look at your life more clearly and see the difference that you would make to your life if the Exceptional Person within you were to be revealed. Don't worry, though, I'm not going to ask you to carry out lots of time-consuming exercises; when I come across those in books I don't do them either! There are just enough to help you look at the particular aspects we are covering at each stage of the book.

You may find that you agree with certain parts of this book but disagree with others, and you may also have further insights to add of your own. It's important to work in the way that you feel the most comfortable with, as long as you address the issues dealt with in the book. Whatever the case I would love to hear from you, as only by sharing such information can we all learn more. If we learn more then we can refine ourselves even further to uncover that Exceptional Person within us all.

You may be reading this and thinking that it is just about navel-gazing and could actually be quite arrogant and self-seeking. But when we find our Exceptional Person within it will not only benefit ourselves but also everyone we encounter in our daily lives.

Paul Ekman, a world-renowned psychologist and expert on non-verbal communication and emotions, studied extraordinary persons and described four qualities found in them, as quoted in Daniel Goleman's book, *Destructive Emotions*. Ekman said: 'Firstly, they emanate a sense of goodness, a palpable quality of being that others notice and agree on. This goodness goes beyond some fuzzy, warm aura and reflects the integrity of the true person.' Ekman also found that in extraordinary people 'there is a transparency between their personal and public life, unlike many charismatics, who have wonderful public lives and rather deplorable personal ones'. This, for Ekman, differentiates the extraordinary person from the charlatan.

Selflessness was the second quality found by Ekman. He noted that extraordinary people are inspiring in their lack of concern about status, fame or ego. They are totally unconcerned whether their position or importance is recognised. Such a lack of egoism, Ekman added, 'from the psychological viewpoint, is remarkable'.

The third quality is a compelling personal presence that others find nourishing. 'People want to be around them because it feels good – though they can't explain why', writes Ekman. The Dalai Lama offers an obvious example of this third quality: the standard Tibetan title is not 'Dalai Lama' but rather *Kundun*, which in Tibetan means 'presence'.

The fourth quality possessed by such extraordinary individuals is 'amazing powers of attentiveness and concentration'. Here again, Ekman found the Dalai Lama exemplary. As Ekman later put it,

In most scientific meetings, I and others who speak frankly readily acknowledge that our mind drifts. As you listen to someone talk, you think about where you are having dinner, your attention comes back to the talk for a few minutes, and then your mind drifts off to your own work and some experiment the discussion inspires. But when I sat with the Dalai Lama for five days in meetings, I noted that His Holiness did not miss a beat. He is one of the closest listeners I have ever encountered – he's totally concentrated. And it's contagious: When I spent those five days with him, amazingly, my mind rarely drifted for a second.[1]

Amazing, or what?

I have used the title, *The Handbook for Exceptional People*, even though I know that we are usually the ones to put ourselves down and not believe that we are indeed exceptional. Through the work that I carry out I find that the common denominator is the same, whether I am working with a CEO of a large FTSE company or someone who has been abused as a child; you will have to read on to find out what that common denominator is.

So, before we begin, I want you to know that I believe you are an Exceptional Person and that you need to look at the layers of information and experience that distorts this fact and then ask yourself what benefit there is in holding on to these layers in your life any longer.

I have split the book into three main sections:

Part I: The Lie of the Land

This is the start of the process. Before we make a move it is imperative that we see where we are starting from and look at the misinformation that we have been telling ourselves and bringing into all the different areas of our lives. Although this may be uncomfortable, it is essential that you work through the process in a thorough way to ensure success. Once this is complete you will be able to move on to the next stage.

Part II: The Human Being

It is usually when we begin to interact with others that things might start to go awry. As we tend not to operate well in complete isolation, it is in our 'being' rather that our 'doing' that we will be effective with others. By this I mean that we are human beings not human doings! Getting this aspect right will be the next step before you are able to enter the final stage.

Part III: Alchemy

Once you have understood the reasons behind making certain decisions or reacting in a particular way in the past, you will be able to choose to refine your behaviour so that you can reap endless rewards in all areas of your life and achieve a life you are truly happy with. These refining traits will provide you with an endless treasure, and as this is an ongoing cyclical process it will form an ever-upward spiral.

The Lie of the Land

The Lie of the Land

Before we can discover how to move forward in our lives we need to understand where we are now.

1. Where are you?

Imagine for a moment that you are walking in mountainous countryside along a narrow path. You are aware of many things: the rocks, trees and bushes that have hindered your progress at times when you had to manoeuvre around them to get to where you currently are. On the distant horizon you can see your destination. You imagine what it is like and long to get there. You are pretty sure how to get there, although you have neither a map nor a guidebook to help you, but you have survived up until now without one, so there is no need. You have heard from others you have met along the way that there may be many dangers ahead of you, but you are confident that you will reach your destination even if you have to take a longer way around.

Suddenly, a thick fog descends on you and your bearings become confused. You spin around a few times trying to recover your bearings, but this only confuses you more, as you are not aware of which direction is which. The map, compass and guidebook now seem an extremely good idea.

The first thing you must do is STOP.

Only when you are 100 per cent confident of where you are, and in which direction your next step should take, will it be safe to move. It may be better to retrace your steps to a place that is safe. You might also need to pick up essential equipment to help you on your journey, and you may even have to learn how to use it competently.

You could, however, choose to stay where you are, although you are unsure of how long the fog will last. Another alternative is to push on in a new direction without any equipment or knowledge of where you are going, and just take a chance.

Just as you are wondering what to do you hear someone approaching. As the walker gets closer you realise that they are a member of the Mountain Rescue Service with all the equipment and knowledge necessary to lead you to a place of safety where you can then assess your options.

The choice is yours: you can either go with them or fend for yourself. However, with darkness closing in and the offer of a comfy resting place, the offer becomes ever more tempting.

In his excellent book *The Road Less Travelled*, M. Scott Peck talks about life as a journey along a narrow path. Looking at a map will show us where we are on this narrow path in relation to other situations and people. This map will be a representation of what is going on in your life.

....

Exercise

STOP. Take time to look at the map of your own life. Look at the different areas of your life in detail:

- Work
- Social life
- Health
- Relationships
- Inner thoughts

1. Imagine that you are doing a documentary on yourself in each of these areas. What would you say to the camera about what you think and how you feel about them?

2. Go back in time and film the key events of your life, both good and bad, and give a running commentary.

Ask yourself, 'What is really going on here?' Which are the areas of your life that you are most comfortable spending time thinking about, and which ones are you the least happy about?

....

So, how's it looking? For many people it will be, 'Life is good, *but* …'. This *but* may be the word that we use only when we are alone. The reality is that we may think and feel that we are not being true to ourselves and that our life is a sham. Is life really good? Or do you feel that you are just existing rather than living?

....

Exercise

Take time to make a note of the positive and negative areas of your life, and as we work through the book take the time to look at how you can change those negative aspects to positives. See overleaf.

....

Positives

_____

_____

_____

_____

_____

_____

_____

_____

_____

_____

_____

_____

_____

Negatives

_____

_____

_____

_____

_____

_____

_____

_____

_____

_____

_____

_____

_____

How did you find this exercise? For some of you it was probably easy. You were able to identify exactly how things were. Others may have found it more tricky, as there are probably a number of areas in your life that you feel ambiguous about. Whichever is the case the next chapter will help you to look at things carefully.

Using a Tool Kit

As our lives become busier so our minds speed up. As we go faster so our eyes have to focus on what lies ahead. The faster we go, the more important it is to focus on where we are going so that we do not collide with anything. This will mean that as we go faster so our field of vision narrows and we become unaware of the nuggets of gold that litter our paths. The nuggets of gold are opportunities that we have not been aware of before, because of the speed in which we have been living our lives.

You may remember an exercise from your schooldays where you took a circular piece of card and divided it into segments. The segments were coloured in with the colours of the spectrum. Then the circle was spun very quickly and the colours disappeared, leaving a white circle. Only by slowing the circle down would the colours gradually begin to reappear, and eventually the individual colours could clearly be seen.

Take time to look at your life and see where things have become very black and white. Do you think it is time to bring back some of the colour by slowing down?

These can be as simple as understanding what someone is saying to us rather than interpreting what we think they are saying because we are no longer bringing preconceptions from our past with us. We can then enjoy a non-judgmental relationship where we are more accepting of others. By behaving differently this may cause others to act differently, too, so that we will achieve an enhanced end result every time.

Emotions also play a major role in our thinking and they can significantly alter the way we view any situation. By taking the emotional aspect out of a situation we are more likely to be able to see things more clearly.

Tool Kit

As you look at the various issues raised in this book, use the following visual tool to help you slow down and take the emotion out of a situation:

You have a sealed jar of water on your desk that has a thin layer of mud sitting at the bottom. Standing out of this layer of mud, fixed to the bottom of the jar, is a 5-carat D flawless

diamond. Its beauty is even more apparent with the backdrop of the mud and it seems to shine in the clear water.

Now imagine shaking the jar so that the clear water becomes stirred up and murky. The diamond can be seen no more.

Now place the jar back on the table, and as time passes so the mud particles slow down and float back to the bottom of the jar. As this happens you begin to be aware of the diamond's shape, and then, only when all the mud particles have settled, are you able to see the brilliance of the diamond once again.

Our minds are no different. Until we take time out to slow our minds down we are unable to see clearly what actually lies before us. Use this tool throughout the book and in your life, and see the treasures that emerge.

Remember: if you fail to stop and reflect, each step that you take may be leading you further away from the place where you finally want to be.

2. Reality

'Ignorance is bliss.' As this quote suggests, ignorance may appear to be for the best, but in reality it ultimately leads to unhappiness at some level. When we are ignorant we are divorced from reality, and in the absence of reality there is delusion. Delusion, as the Buddhist doctrine suggests, is a poison that can contaminate our mind.

Our mind is a very powerful tool that, at present, we do not fully understand. Yet, it has the ability to construct certain information in such a way that it distorts reality and protects us from any pain. Once a comfortable pattern of coping has been established, and a defence mechanism is in place, every interaction that we have can be affected in some way. This will most likely happen in an unconscious lightning-quick way that will be strengthened each time the pattern is set in motion.

This may seem a little dramatic. How can one area of our life affect, and be transmitted to, everything we do?

....

Exercise

Picture a pure white rug. Imagine weaving in just one strand of red thread through the length of the rug. It doesn't matter how you look at the rug, your eyes will always see that strand of red. It always affects the way the rug appears.

The way that we interact with others is no different. So much of our communication with others is done unconsciously (that strand of red woven into the rug is always there and always affects the way the rug appears, whichever way we look at it), and our unconscious beliefs or feelings will be shown as different personality traits that communicate to others what we are feeling beneath the surface.

Our mind will always create the reality that we want it to. This can distort what is really happening to such a level that it is difficult to see any other way. The more we use the same pattern the more it will become ingrained into who we are, and the quicker we will be able to access it.

Imagine a wire being tightly wrapped around a beam. With each turn around the beam the wire goes further along the beam and, therefore, further away from its starting point. And because it is tightly wound the further it moves away the more difficult it is to unwind. See below:

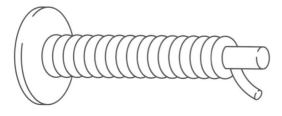

Getting back to the source

This is where the hard work begins. In order to change the way that we see things now (reality) and, therefore, so that we can make informed and correct decisions in the future, we have to go back to the beginning. Only then can we understand why we see things in a certain way – in other words the 'source' of how we see things.

The old mechanisms will continue to operate until you return to the source, and the longer you leave it the more wire you will have to uncoil.

Imagine a tree that produces leaves that are not healthy because it is growing in poor soil. If you trim the top of the tree the leaves will grow back in the same way. The only way to treat the problem is to deal with what is going on at the roots by improving the soil around them or feeding them. This will improve the health of the leaves.

We have many examples in our lives where there are different views of reality. By just watching the news and reading the papers from around the world we can see that the same news story is reported in many different ways with often very different conclusions and results; for example, many of us will be able to recall the different sides of the Iraqi war as portrayed by Western news channels and Aljazeera. So how can we ever know when we have reached ultimate reality? The answer is we will not, as it will only ever be *our*

interpretation of reality. This interpretation of reality is governed by the use of filters within our mind.

Filters are created by the mind in order to protect us at all levels. They control what we actually see and will, therefore, determine what actions we take as a result. We use these filters in every situation in our lives. Our minds employ them at breakneck speed to ensure that there is conformity and continuity in our minds. This conformity and continuity tell us that we are OK because it has had previous knowledge of a similar situation where we have survived and it knows that it has the ability to enable us to survive again.

When we experience a particular situation we often work out the result that we want to achieve in advance, either consciously or unconsciously, and this is usually based on something we have previously experienced. We then work towards achieving that outcome. However, this might have disastrous affects, which produce the same result time and time again.

Do you often find yourself asking the question, 'Why does this always happen to me?' The reason the same outcome occurs is because our brain has built a filter during earlier circumstances that seemed entirely appropriate at the time, but is now outdated and is not appropriate; for example, we may have created a filter as a child and not checked to see whether that it is appropriate to use it within our current lives, or we may not have dealt with the issues that surrounded that earlier event. Your choice now is whether you want to change this filter in your mind so that you will deal with similar issues differently in the future.

Finding patterns

Begin by looking at recurring patterns in your life. They may be on a very superficial level, or, more pertinently, on a deeper level; for example, you might ask, 'Why do all my relationships end up this way?'

Within this cycle the only thing that we can control is ourselves, our perception of reality and our actions. The conformity and continuity works as follows:

Our minds want certainty and go about creating equations so that they can constantly prove or disprove what is taking place. The interesting thing is that we are usually very young when our minds create these equations and, therefore, by the time we reach adulthood some of these elements might not be that useful yet we are often blissfully unaware of this!

Let's look at the example of the young mind that created the following equation $x = y + z$. Once the mind has created this it will always want to prove x is equal to the components y + z. Let's take the example of a child who has grown up with a parent who was showing the love through giving them lots of cuddles but was also an alcoholic. When the parent had been drinking and the child was around they would receive more cuddles and reinforced their feelings by telling the child "I love you". One possible equation that could be created is x (love) = y (cuddles) + z (alcohol). Here love can only exist in the presence of alcohol. Is it any surprise that the child of the alcoholic parent has grown up and either become an alcoholic themselves or attracted a partner who is.

Note: this is not always the case – they may decide that they do not want to have alcohol in their lives at all.

Therefore, only by unlearning this equation and learning a new one where x (love) = y (cuddles) at the exclusion of z (alcohol) can a new and healthier life begin.

Now do you have an understanding why people may find change so difficult? The brain is always seeking to prove itself right, through what it already knows – not what it doesn't know.

....

Exercise

So let's take a look back at the path you having been travelling along until now. Look at the people who have been in your life and their importance. Look for patterns, similarities and coincidences in people, events and feelings, however silly they may appear.

....

What have you found? Now here is the interesting thing: you will have been responsible for creating and fulfilling all of these situations yourself at some level. Although we can't be responsible for experiences that happened to us as children we are responsible for allowing them to colour the way we deal with situations now. The uncomfortable feelings that often go along with these memories, especially when the result is not the one you would want, are in your control.

The old adage that if we do the same things in the same way we will always get the same result stands up ($x = y + z$).

Dealing with the reality of these situations and looking at the beliefs created by them is key to being exceptional. There will be many reasons as to why we are choosing to create the reality that we do. At the moment you may be thinking,

'Well, this is just the way I am.' I would challenge this by saying, 'This is the way you have chosen to be, based on the information that you had available at the time.' By saying this it opens up the possibility for another way of living.

Once we have a clear view of reality, and know where we are, we can then look at how far away we are from the path that we want to be travelling on.

Although we cannot go back and re-live our past lives we can look back at the beliefs we have picked up and created along the way that have brought us to where we are, and we can consider ways of changing these from the root so that in the future we can choose a different course of action that will produce a different result – one that we want.

The problems in looking back

Looking back at your past may be uncomfortable for you because your past may hold many events that you find painful and uncomfortable to deal with. You may also believe that you have dealt with your past and have decided that that's just the way things were. In my experience, however, both personally and professionally, if you feel this way you are hindering yourself from living the life that you truly want.

You may wish to seek professional help from a counsellor or a therapist in dealing with your past, and I would encourage you wholeheartedly to do so. They will help you unpack and explore the difficult areas of your life in a safe and supportive environment.

3. Understanding your past

Your past, and the beliefs that you have constructed around it, have made you the person you are today. Exceptional People will look at the reality of these beliefs and realise which ones need to be altered so that they can produce the outcome they desire in the future.

Whether we like it or not, the psychotherapist Sigmund Freud (1856-1939), and others, were right in proposing that much of our life is determined by the time we are seven or eight years old, hence the Jesuit saying: 'Give me the boy when he is seven, and I will show you the man.'

But what is it that has been determined, and can it be changed? Or are we confined within the prison of 'You can't teach an old dog new tricks' and 'A leopard cannot change its spots'?

Let's look at how beliefs may manifest themselves. Take the simple example of a little girl who is in the kitchen with her mother. Suddenly the mother sees a spider skitter across the floor. She quickly picks up her daughter, stands on a chair and starts to scream with terror. The little girl is being sent the message that spiders are dangerous and scary, and should be avoided at all costs for safety reasons.

So guess what happens next time the little girl sees a spider? Her brain will tell her there is a spider in front of her and it will access the correct mechanism in dealing with such a creature. Whoosh! Stand on a chair and scream, as this will keep me safe. Spiders are to be avoided at all costs.

It is clear to see where this belief began and it is a simple example. Now imagine the effect of a child growing up in a house where their father hits their mother. The message that is being created for the child here is that when you get frustrated and do not agree with someone else, especially a woman, part of that frustration can manifest itself through using physical abuse. The child will also receive the message that hitting is part of a relationship. Different beliefs may arise within girls and boys who have lived through these experiences, yet both will experience disastrous effects.

It is hardly any wonder that we see these patterns repeated later in life where the child has turned into the abuser or the abused.

Through such an experience a child may come to believe that this kind of behaviour is one of the ingredients that makes up a relationship ($x = y + z$). As a result their mind will justify the abuse, as it fits into the overall picture of a relationship – the abuser was also often the carer and lover. This is where the tainting occurs; the thread is introduced, and it influences every decision that we make in the future without us realising it.

How we react

Even when we reach a situation that actually meets our desired needs, but without the negative element – in this case the abuse – we feel uncomfortable there, as it does not correspond to the pattern that we know. We then take steps to remove ourselves from this situation or force a new situation so that the flawed pattern can be satisfied. Because we are usually unable to see the true meaning and root of this uncomfortable feeling, we prefer instead to interpret it to mean that it is not good for us. The good situation challenges our old beliefs and is not 'good' for them although it is good for us, but because we know only the old tainted belief we want to confirm it. Therefore, if a new healthy situation takes place it does not conform to that old belief and is rejected. The cycle is therefore strengthened and restarted and we move further along the road away from reality, and another coil of wire is laid down on that beam.

Looking at abuse as a belief is obviously very extreme, yet it does highlight how good the mind is, even under awful conditions, in constructing a path through which it can create conformity and continuity, therefore ensuring survival.

I feel strongly that all of our beliefs, however severe or tame, will affect our overall character and behaviour at some level. Therefore, it is key to look at our past to see the root of our beliefs. Only this way can we begin to unlearn those damaging beliefs and begin to change our patterns of behaviour so that we can experience different results in the future.

Although we cannot change our past we can look back and see what we can choose to do differently in the future when we face a similar situation. By reacting differently in the future we can expect the outcome of the new situation to be different from the way similar situations have worked out in the past.

As mentioned earlier, there may be those of you that have had very traumatic pasts – please do not underestimate the effects that these incidents have had on your entire life. Every relationship on every level will have been affected. There will be a deep unease within you that only you will be aware of at some level. You probably keep this well hidden behind locked steel doors that are impenetrable. Take time to acknowledge this place and know that you are not alone in being there. Know that with the right kind of care and attention you can leave this prison and move to a new, free life that is not controlled by fear. If you do not feel ready to face this reality now then I suggest you put this book down rather than building up defence mechanisms as you work through it. This will simply take you further away from where you eventually wish to be. Pick it up again when you have the courage and support to do so.

Where did our beliefs originate?

For those people who have had a pleasant and happy past there will be, nevertheless, certain beliefs that you have cultivated that are not always helping you to achieve the results that you want. Look at whose beliefs you really hold. In most cases, they are from our perception of how our parents operated.

Our levels of conscious awareness will play a huge role in this process. As with doing any activity that we now do unconsciously, like driving a car after we have been driving for a number of years, it is only by becoming consciously aware that we can begin to look at the reality of how many bad habits we have picked up.

4. The present

So here we are in the present; our brains are working unconsciously at around 97 per cent, living out our lives in the way we know best. Imagine, however, that the decisions you are making are tainted in some way by your past. Think back and look at the path you have travelled along to this point – just one degree out from the start can have very interesting results years down the road.

A word of warning to the strong-minded: unless you deal with the reality of your past now you will continue to take yourself off-track, as your past still has a hold over your life. Many of you will be sitting behind a protective wall ensuring that life conforms to the pattern you have formed within your mind. If you find yourself thinking in this way then STOP and see the lie of the land. Carrying on the way you are will not accomplish the real results that you want. You will continue to have that frustrated feeling within you until you realise that you cannot control everything and that what taught you to behave this way is linked to an event somewhere in your past.

A story for the strong-minded to consider:

The Captain of a US warship saw an object appear on his radar during a foggy night at sea. Immediately he signalled it to move aside. The reply came back of 'NO, you move aside'. The Captain, with more determination and superiority, said 'NO, you move aside, we are the US Naval Fleet and have many ships within our battle group'. The reply came back, 'NO, you move aside, we are a lighthouse'!

Assuming you are definitely right and that there is nothing in your past that you need to deal with could have disastrous outcomes and you could find your life running aground.

Unconscious choices

Every action and reaction will have its root in a learned belief. Some of these beliefs will work well whereas others will not. It is healthy to look at all of our beliefs as and when they come up. In this way we can bring our unconscious thoughts, beliefs and actions into the conscious mind. As we do this we may be surprised at our findings.

The four stages of learning that we all go through are universal. Look at the diagram below:

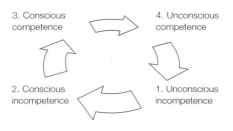

3. Conscious competence

4. Unconscious competence

2. Conscious incompetence

1. Unconscious incompetence

Most of us when we reach the last stage of Unconscious Competence stop just there. This is where the bad habits that we have picked up remain and often get worse. Look at our experience in how we have learned to drive or play a sport. Before we started driving, for example, we were in the Unconscious Incompetence stage where we don't know that we don't know we can't drive. As we start lessons we are aware that we make mistakes and would be unsafe to take to the roads alone. This is the Conscious Incompetence stage. This stage can feel quite uncomfortable as we keep making mistakes. As we carry on we gain competence and enter the Conscious Competence stage. Here we are aware of our actions and know that we are making the correct decisions. It is after this stage, in which we usually pass our test, that we then start driving and become less consciously aware of what we are doing, and we can quite easily hold conversations while eating a chocolate bar and gesticulating at the driver who has just cut us up! Welcome to Unconscious Competence.

This is the point in the cycle where you can start to pick up bad habits. Initially they creep in and sit there and we are oblivious to their existence. They will remain there and often grow larger until our conscious awareness, or that of someone else's, picks them up on the radar. We are then faced with the choice of whether or not we want to change our behaviour. If we do we will go through the cycle again and teach ourselves back to a position of Conscious Competence.

The driving example keeps it all very safe and away from an emotive subject. Now relate that to how we relate to others and ourselves. As children the journey from Unconscious Incompetence to Unconscious Competence is very short in both time and distance, as the driving force within us to survive creates beliefs in a blink of an eye. This can be explained further, if you want to, by looking into child development psychology. Some basic belief structures can be shown by the following simple example: much of what we do today was learned as a child.

How many times do you find yourself using exactly the same phrases as your parents in all kinds of situations? Even when we look at our actions and how similar they are to our parents' we are often surprised.

Language

Now let's look a little deeper at the words we use. If you listen very carefully to the words that you, and others, use you will be able to pick up much information about what is going on under the surface. In very simple terms we can either use positive or negative language and this will affect how we communicate with each other both consciously and unconsciously. If a person tends to use negative language then they will be more likely to have a negative experience of life than a person who chooses to use positive language.

To highlight this I turn to a fantastic little book called *My Little Book of Verbal Antidotes* by Georges Philips and Tony Jennings. It highlights words that we use in our everyday language and explores the negative impact that it can have within our lives. Thankfully, it also provides positive alternatives to give us a positive outcome. Here are the words:

Toxic words

Verbal antidotes

Problem

A problem is the difference between what you have and what you want. The problem is the current solution. Everything is just a situation. Only see a situation in a way that would allow you to seek better situations.

Solution

The problem is in effect the solution. So what is the problem? Surely it is to find a better way of dealing with the situation. The greatest gift we can give ourselves is to see everything as an opportunity to make something better, so that nothing is a problem, rather a situation that can be improved.

Can't

The mind says 'yes' to whatever you say it can't do. The mind is instructed not to bother looking for a solution, as it doesn't exist.

Can/won't

Say a sentence with either 'can' or 'won't' and it will give power to the statement and will give it a different meaning and intention.

Wish

A wish is what the heart wants that the mind believes it does not deserve. Wishing is wasting.

A well-constructed sentence that seeks solutions. Replace wish thoughts with how thoughts.

Don't

The mind takes a negative and makes it happen.

Be clear about what you do want. Convert all sentences into a positive statement of what is desired rather than what is not desired.

Why

Unless you want the same experience, you have no need to know why. We need not know why everything happens. 'Why' confirms and perpetuates a belief.

How

Using 'how' asks the mind to look for a solution.

Try

The mind only knows how to say 'yes' to every request. So when we say 'do it', it does. When we say 'try it', it does. When we hear others say that they will 'try' to do something, we need to be aware of what they mean.

Will/can/do

This eliminates any trying and creates doing. This also removes any element of failure, it only creates outcomes/results.

Truth

Whenever we use truth words ('honestly', 'it's true', and so on) we are implying that there are times when we are not being true and honest. Truth is usually only a temporary fact.

Be plain, straightforward, honest and believable. Stop using these words to defend what you know to be true.

But

The mind focuses on what follows on from 'but' and dismisses, deletes, and erases the rest.

And

By eliminating 'but' or replacing it with 'and' creates a much more positive statement.

Should
Implies that we are aware
we are not doing some-
thing we had planned
to do. 'Should' precedes
a silent 'but'.

Will/can/do
Avoid justifying your
decisions for doing or
saying something.

Always and never
The use of these and
similar words prevent you
from seeing possible
alternatives.

Be specific. Being specific
reduces the risk of infecting
the system with generalis-
ations that form patterns.

Doubt
Doubt prevents the joy
of expectation. Doubt
promotes negative
possibilities.

Will/can/do
Remove doubt and you
create optimistic and
pleasurable possibilities.

Or
Limits choice. Stops the
mind from seeking other
solutions.

Remove it and you open
up options. You can use it
to limit the options of others.

Coincidence
Random happenings in the world neither wait for nor depend upon human understanding.

Think of a possible reason instead. It's OK not to know. Accept that some things happen for the benefit of others and are not always meant for you.

Is, are and am
Restricts other details being taken into consideration and even negates further information being sought.

Be context specific to allow for other options.

No
It is easily misinterpreted as total rejection.

Be specific about what you are saying 'no' to. It is useful to learn to be more specific about what exactly we do not want to do.[2]

These words can have effects that run throughout the whole of our lives that we often ignore, or, more worryingly, do not even notice. It is as if everything we do is tainted in some way by the words that come out of our mouths.

The words that we use can also shine the light on what is going on at a much deeper level. People will often pre-frame a sentence with a small throwaway phrase that tells us so much more. Let's take the example of the phrase 'I'm afraid I …'. Although this may come across as being relatively innocuous it creates a seed of fear that can propagate through everything we do. By creating a thought of fear, the number of choices open to us is dramatically reduced. You may be reading this and saying to yourself, 'What a load of rubbish.' However, the reason I can be sure of it is that it was a phrase that I often used myself. It was an indication of the fear that was burning deep within me that I managed not to notice consciously and, more importantly, I had locked away.

I find interactions with people fascinating, and even when I listen to someone's answerphone message I find myself listening out for clues to what is potentially going on for that individual. Have a go yourself – you may be surprised by what you find.

By looking at the list of words above you can see that they all have an impact. Just by using the alternative words you will create a different outcome.

If you are still unsure of the deep power of words then I would like you to carry out the following:

....

Exercise

1. Ask a colleague or friend to hold out their strongest arm in front of them.

2. Ask them to say the word STRONG five times and to adopt their 'strong' face.

3. Now ask them to resist you attempting to push their arm back down – use your full hand when doing this.

4. Then ask them to repeat the exercise but this time using the word WEAK instead and adopting their 'weak' face.

5. Use just one finger when you push down on their arm.

....

Confusing?

At the earliest stage in our life we have learned that weak means 'not strong'. It is as if our whole body has learned this and just gives up with futile resistance.

In an interesting experiment that took place in the US (in the days when such experiments were not required to go before the ethical committees) a group of schoolchildren were split randomly, irrespective of intelligence and ability, into two groups. One group was told that they were the brighter set and the others were told that they were below standard. Can you guess the outcome? The majority of the first group excelled in studies and in life, whereas those in the second group did not.

Now put this into context once again with your own past. The effect of many events can have lasting and damaging results at a level that we are unconsciously aware of. So, once again, I am going to ask you to STOP and think about your past to see if there is something that needs to be addressed.

So how can we begin to change things? This will be discussed in the next section.

5. Conscious awareness

What is conscious awareness? Your conscious awareness is allowing you to read these words at the moment. There will be other things going on around you that you are also aware of. Sometimes you will find yourself so consumed by what you are doing that you will miss what is going on in the background. This difference in the levels of conscious awareness is key if you are to grow as an Exceptional Person. Yes, there will be times when your full attention is required, especially if you are carrying out very precise procedures – the consequences of not attending fully at those times could result in calamity. Yet it is important to enlarge your area of focus as often as possible and to look at the reality of what is going on around you. Although your actions might appear at the time to be the right ones, other people may perceive them as totally offensive.

By expanding your area of focus you will be aware of others' reality. By giving yourself this enlarged picture you will potentially be able to see why certain interactions are so difficult and always end in disaster.

Also, if you are going to change your behaviour you will have to make some choices. So instead of carrying on in the same way, initially you will have to be consciously aware so that the hard-wired programme within you does not take over and you can choose another way. This will produce a different result – I promise.

Becoming more consciously aware is imperative if you are to learn how to uncover the Exceptional Person within you. I am not saying that we must become consciously aware of everything, as we would not be able to function if we did this. Current studies in psychology indicate that we are able to have only seven (plus or minus two) items within our conscious awareness at any one time and, although we would not get very far if we were consciously aware of breathing in and out every time, this is a good place to return to in order to slow the mind down and clear it altogether.

6. Slowing down

Take the next two minutes to carry out this simple exercise:

....

Exercise

1. Just close your eyes and concentrate on breathing in and out for two minutes. Focus on this and this only. Take time to notice the rise and fall of your chest, the pulling in of your stomach and the air passing in and out of your nostrils and mouth. When you think two minutes is up open your eyes.

2. Now be consciously aware of everything you do in the coming minutes – especially be aware of any interaction with others.

....

You may be surprised that you did not actually take two minutes. The first time I did this exercise with 500 management consultants I got them to do it for one minute, asking them to put their hand up when they thought the time was up, the first hand went up after 25 seconds!

This is a clear example of how we spend much of our time speeding things up. As situations are speeded up our field of vision begins to narrow. Imagine travelling on a train and looking out of the window. As the train starts it is easy to see what is happening on the platform. As the train reaches its maximum speed and travels through another station, where it does not stop, it is very difficult to see what is happening on that platform.

When you enter into a situation now, try to move at a slower pace and observe what is going on; become more consciously aware of others and yourself. See what effect your words and behaviour have on others – is it positive or negative? By slowing down you will also be aware of the nuggets of gold that are strewn along the sides of your path, which until now have gone unnoticed because your field of vision has been too narrow.

You may be aware that when you interact with certain people it is not exactly plain sailing. You might feel that you don't quite get on with each other or are not on the same wavelength, or perhaps you just feel a little uncomfortable with them. As you become consciously aware of these

interactions you will be able to make a choice. You can either do what you would normally do and receive the same outcome as usual, or you can choose to do something different and see what happens.

Initially, this has the potential to be uncomfortable for you, as you will be stepping into new territory and there may be an element of fear that creeps in. The chances are, though, that by doing something different you will have a different outcome – be consciously aware of it and check to see whether you like it. If you don't experience a different outcome, carry out something different until you achieve a result that you are happy with and that is a win-win situation for both parties. Here is an example: you know that person in your office you have always struggled to get on with? Have a go at changing your initial interaction with them until you get the result that you want. Instead of just saying, 'Morning' as you walk past their desk, you could try saying, 'Morning Bob, how are things?' and take some time to stop and talk to him. It is the small changes that can often bring about the big shifts in the outcome – just think about how powerful the rudder of a ship is in influencing something that is much larger.

As you spend more time in this slower and more consciously aware state your ability to see reality will increase.

WARNING: as soon as you think you are seeing reality and becoming smug with yourself you will have stepped into the realm of arrogance, where reality becomes an illusion! So always be careful to keep both feet firmly on the ground.

Keep a journal

The more reality you see may, at times, surprise and shock you. I urge you to keep a rein on this new-found wisdom for now, but one useful thing you can do is to start keeping a journal. Here you will be able to record your thoughts and observations in a way that is safe. As we become aware of new things, others often do not. They will be used to seeing us in a certain way, and when we change they often do not accept the change, as it does not conform to their definition of who we are or the way things are to them. A journal allows us to note thoughts down without disrupting the tightly held beliefs of others.

One of the key aspects to remember is to take time out to STOP and slow down. Our lives are like hurricanes that often carry on at 100+ mph. In the centre of each hurricane is an eye where there is a massive decrease in pressure and no wind. The forces of nature cause everything to move out of this eye. Your task is to keep inside it, where you will find peace. Without an eye there is no hurricane – without peace there will be no you.

7. The future

Just take time to reflect; sit down on your path and reflect. You have now stepped into a unique place where you have your world and life before you. Every decision you have made to date has been your decision, whether you were consciously, or unconsciously, aware of it. And guess what: you are in control of every decision you will make from now on and for the rest of your life.

Are you happy with where you are on your path?

If you are not happy then you have the freedom, and the power, to choose how to change your current position and move to a place where you would like to be. Although this might appear daunting, the remainder of the book will begin to show you how, as an Exceptional Person, you can further accomplish what you want.

This is a good place to STOP again and to look to see if there is still anything that you are not prepared to look at or deal with from your past. This is also the time to look at all of the areas of your life and decide what you want. You cannot, and should not attempt to, control every situation; you can only control yourself. The key is to concentrate on BEING rather than DOING. If you DO then you will be speeding up – if you BE then you will be the authentic you with everyone around you, and this will bring you unlimited treasures: an ability to see each situation more clearly and without preconceptions and to communicate with others in a way that is non-judgemental, fair and true, opening up endless possibilities for lasting and rewarding relationships.

8. Testing and pushing

As I have indicated already the mind likes to have clarity. In order to do this it creates a set of beliefs that it will aim to prove correct in order to protect you and to make sure that you survive.

The greater the pain that is associated with the belief at the time of its creation, the greater the need will be to prove the belief in order to protect yourself. When you relate to others you often have a tendency to push hard at proving yourself correct and make sure that nothing stands in your way, even if this is to your own detriment.

As you can imagine this can have disastrous effects – it can be like a tornado ripping through a shanty town. The energy that might be put into confirming a belief can be amazing, and you can sometimes sense the nervousness within the person during this process. It is almost as if nothing else matters.

For that person, even when all is apparently quiet and calm, because the need in their mind to prove the belief they hold is so strong the tornado will whip itself up to produce the calamity that the tainted belief requires. Being in a relationship with someone like this is understandably tiring, and it is impossible to sustain without damaging both parties.

Be aware of when you are testing and pushing a situation to reinforce the reality that you have created in your life. You may notice that when you do this your mind speeds up and your vision narrows to focus on your goal.

Back to basics

So how would the Exceptional Person deal with this pattern within themselves? Going back to basics you have to STOP and take a look at the reality of what you are doing and what is driving your actions. Look at the diagram below:

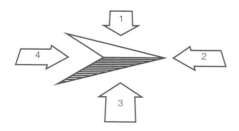

Imagine you are standing in position 1. What do you see? Now put yourself in the other three positions and describe what you see. Whose view is right? Well, from their own different positions they all are. So in this situation four different people can be looking at the same object and all see very different things.

You can possibly see how having a discussion about what each person sees and who is right could end up in disagreement. They might naturally believe that they were right and that the rest of you were wrong, and no amount of discussion (or argument) would change their mind. Only by taking time out to understand what the others might be seeing will each person be able to understand the other's belief.

....

Exercise

Look at areas in your own life where there might be disagreement about a certain topic. Take time to repeat this exercise from each angle and see what a difference this can make. This will enable you to see how others might view a certain action, event or situation.

....

Although their point of view may be very alien to your way of thinking it is highly likely that there will be someone out there who does indeed hold that view. Test these views and see what works for you.

Then comes the clincher:

- Either just accept them – they are all right;
- or just imagine accepting them. How much stress suddenly evaporates?

Yes, those people might be deluding themselves, but does that affect who you are? This is unlikely, although if you have a relationship with a person who holds these views and you are looking for a win-win situation then further discussions will need to take place; the other person may then have to be introduced to the concept of looking at things from other angles as well.

If both of you stop pushing against each other, then your vision will improve, as you will have both slowed down and taken time to understand the viewpoint of the other person. As Steven Covey says in his book *The 7 Habits of Highly Effective People*, 'Seek first to understand before being understood.'[3] In this way you will be able to be more open to creating the win-win situation from the start and this will make life infinitely easier.

9. Attachment and aversion

In much of my early work I frequently met people who had an all-or-nothing mindset, where everything was either black or white and nothing could exist in between. This all-or-nothing mindset could be described as a binary thought process, using either 0 or 1. I was amazed at the speed people arrived at either 0 or 1 – it was nothing short of lightning quick!

I found that usually something in their childhood had triggered off this way of thinking. Some writers have linked this kind of behaviour to very early childhood. Here is what one writer has said about attachment:

However, the clinical importance of these bonds was not fully appreciated until John Bowlby introduced the concept of attachment in a report on the effects of [parental] deprivation (Bowlby, 1951). Bowlby (1969) postulated that the pattern of an infant's early attachment to parents would form the basis for all later social relationships. On the basis of his experience with disturbed children, he hypothesised that, when the parent was unavailable or only partially available during the first months of the child's life, the attachment process would be interrupted, leaving enduring emotional scars and predisposing a child to behavioural problems.[4]

That might appear to be a little severe, so let me expand. When a child is born there is a natural bond with the parents, especially the mother. If the mother and/or the father is absent, or does not spend a great deal of time with the child, the child looks for an attachment similar to the one it had while in the womb. Because the child has a space in their life they have an urgent need to find someone to attach to. Later, as an older child or adult, this person may be so keen to seek and make friends with others that it is almost overwhelming and pressurising in the process. And this can be carried into the workplace, too, where the person needs to make a connection with a client to make a deal (the obvious place for someone like this would perhaps be in a sales environment).

Now, let's look at aversion. If you watch a baby with a parent who is continually doting on it, or abusing it, the baby will decide after a while that it has had enough of the attention or abuse and will push it away or withdraw. The overcaring or abusive parent is often distraught at this point and keeps on pushing, but receives a more marked response from the baby. As the child grows up their parent continues to be overprotective or abusive and, as earlier patterns have been learned, the child pushes that help and support away, or shrinks away from the abuse.

By the time the child becomes an adult they become an exceptionally independent, self-sufficient person who thinks that they are just fine by themselves.

Neither process is healthy. Because the person has learned from an early age how to cope with these situations, when any new situation arises they react in an extreme way in the quickest time possible to create certainty and safety for themselves. The idea that there can be anything in between is too scary.

However, please do not use this as an excuse to blame your parents for everything that has happened in your life. Remember that at the root of this is something that is in your hands: choice.

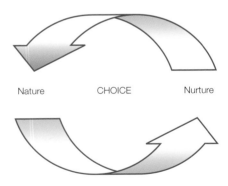

Nature   CHOICE   Nurture

Moving on

Understanding how to change is about learning a new way of seeing things and realising that there may be something in between the extremes of black and white in which life can exist and flourish. Just by allowing yourself to take time when making a decision will enable colour to seep into the picture. Once a person is in this new place a whole host of new possibilities can emerge.

This is where a more balanced perspective can flourish and an individual can just be.

If we have been honest with ourselves as we have worked through this book so far we should now find that the reality of our own situation has become much clearer. We can now take up the title of Human Being and move on to the next stage.

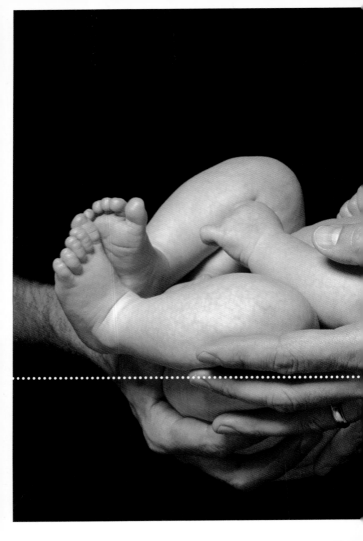

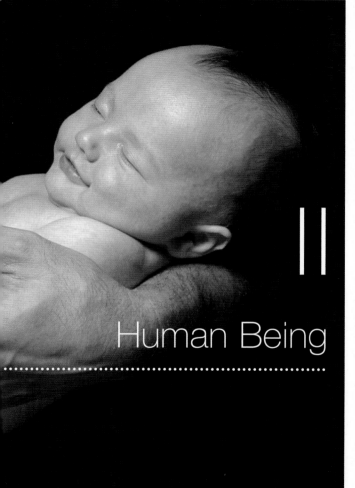

II

Human Being

Human Being

Now that you have taken on the title of Human Being it is time to look at yourself a little deeper before we turn to the world around us.

1. Relationship

Notice from the start that the title of this chapter is 'Relationship' and not 'Relationships'. Unless you understand your primary relationship the relationships that you have will be a fraction of what they could be.

So what is your primary relationship? If you hadn't guessed it already, it is with yourself.

STOP and think about this:

Your primary relationship is with yourself.

By DOING the whole time you are negating this primary relationship.

So STOP and make an appraisal of your relationship with yourself. Ask yourself the following questions and see how healthy your relationship pyramid is (as shown on the previous page):

- How good at communicating with yourself are you?
- How honest are you with yourself?
- How much do you trust yourself?
- How much respect do you have for yourself?

Communication, at the base of our pyramid, is the basis of any relationship upon which you can build these other attributes. Just imagine the effect of having a narrow block at the base of the pyramid instead of the broad base – the relationship would be very unstable.

One question surrounds all the remaining questions in the list above:

How much love do you have for yourself?

We need to start from a position of loving ourselves. So often we are quick to criticise ourselves and feel disappointment in the way we look, the way we act and how we are succeeding in business or on a personal level; we might feel we are not good enough or compare ourselves unfairly with others. But we need to love ourselves as we are so that we can have the relaxed confidence to move on in our lives and make a good relationship with ourselves and others.

Many of you may be uncomfortable with some of the questions above, especially the last one. Consider the following:

Our relationships are a reflection of who we are.

Your relationships now

Think about the people who are in your life at the moment. At some level you will have attracted them into your life and been attracted to them. This may have happened consciously. The reality of it, however, is that we will have done much of this unconsciously. Some of these people may not be the kind of people we really want in our lives. The questions you must ask yourself therefore are, 'What is it that I am putting out there that is attracting this type of person into my life?' and 'What is stopping me from cutting them out of my life?'

There will also be certain things that annoy you about some of these people and your relationship with them. The question to ask yourself then is, 'When do I exhibit these qualities myself?', because we often find the very things we do ourselves are the most annoying traits in others.

You may be feeling fairly uncomfortable at this point, but the great thing is you have the power, right and opportunity to change your current circumstances. As you become more consciously aware of your actions you will see the situations that cause certain qualities to arise within you.

As you develop a new relationship with yourself you may want to change some things about yourself. There is a saying that encapsulates this: 'Be the love you seek.'

Once you develop the type of love within yourself that you wish and you are simply 'being' this, you will not only start to attract different people but you will also be much more aware of the people that you do not want to attract so that you can take steps to avoid attracting them.

Here is an example: let's say that you want to receive a love that is gentle, caring, compassionate and tender. You will not attract this into your life if you do not embrace those qualities in yourself and others. The reality is that there are times when we might be gentle, caring, compassionate and tender, but there are other times when we are not. The times when we are not will infect the times when we are. If we can deal with the reason behind us not acting in the way that we would like, we will unlock many happy days ahead.

As we speed up our lives, the gentle, caring, compassionate and tender love is distorted and that's what others will see and experience. By slowing down you will reap the benefits of a better relationship with yourself and with those around you.

2. Love

Although love is written about, portrayed in films, painted upon canvas and discussed in minute detail there appears to be a great deal of unhappiness that goes along with it, too. This begs the question, 'This thing that we have found, is it really love?'

The word itself can cause some of us to feel all gooey whereas for others it can cause them to tense up and break into a cold sweat. So what is love?

The Bible tells us in one of the most popular marriage readings: '4*Love is patient, love is kind. It does not envy, it does not boast, it is not proud. 5It is not rude, it is not self-seeking, it is not easily angered, it keeps no record of* *wrongs. ⁶Love does not delight in evil but rejoices with the truth. ⁷It always protects, always trusts, always hopes, always perseveres.'*

⁸Love never fails.

New International Version; 1 Corinthians 13, verses 4 – 8

And there it is! However, although it doesn't seem too difficult, in reality it is. So where is the difficulty?

The first difficulty is in realising what it is that is working against love.

CAUTION: what you are about to learn will transform how you think about things going forward from here.

If you ask people what the opposite of love is, what do you think they will say? They will probably say 'hate'. For most of our lives we have thought that if we do not carry hate with us then we must be loving. This is probably one of the biggest deceptions that the human race lives under.

So what is the opposite of love? It is FEAR.

Love and fear

To keep things simple let's look at things in the following way: everything you do originates either from a root of fear or a root of love. Just STOP and think about that. Everything you do comes from either a root of fear or a root of love.

Sometimes it is beneficial to have a fear within us; for example, if you are in your office and you see a fire, fear is a good thing, as your body goes into survival mode and runs away. However, think about how beneficial it would be in a work situation if your employees were in a state of fear the whole time. Would they be working at their most effective capacity and would their levels of communication be as good as they could be? Unlikely.

Now imagine that you are trying to carry out an action and there is a root fear there; would you be able to carry out that action in the best way? Unlikely.

There are examples in the world where people have been driven by a fear and been very successful as a result. A sad reality, however, is that often they are deeply lonely and unfulfilled, and they worry that they will be discovered to be a fraud. Often they will mask this by spending their money on things that show to others that they are outwardly successful (such as cars, planes, expensive houses, and so on), yet what is happening on the inside is very different.

As we have already discovered, we are unconscious of many of our actions. Think of the impact of this: from my own personal experience I can say that fear was an underlying root in all of my actions. Notice that I say 'all', as there will be a common thread through all my actions. Remember the red thread through the rug?

Now here is the wonderful irony: unconditional love casts out all fear. Unconditional love is the love we hold for someone regardless of what they might do or say. Through this unconditional love we can always be there for them without expectation or judgement.

Think back to one of the earlier quotes: 'Be the love you seek.' You have the ability to cast out all your fear by learning and living the meaning of unconditional love.

Spend some time defining what you view as unconditional love, and what you view as conditional love. In both lists look at each word and see if there is any element of fear contained in the lists, and, more importantly, where specifically this fear comes from within you.

This can be a hard process, especially when we look at the 'imperfect' list and see some of those things in our lives today. From my own personal experience the amount of fear that was there, and at times still is, was discouraging to say the least.

As we all move through our lives we can now look at our actions and see whether each one is performed from a root of love or a root of fear. To remind you of this, carry out the following:

....

Exercise

Imagine placing a golf ball in the palm of each hand. Keep one of your hands open and clench the other hand tightly around the ball. What options do each of the balls have? You may feel more comfortable clenching one of the balls, as it is safe and secure and will not roll anywhere, but what options does it have? The ball in your open hand, however, may feel a little vulnerable but it has infinite opportunities to move freely.

Take time to look at those situations in your own life where you are holding on to things tightly. What possibilities are you missing by doing this? The clenched fist represents the root of fear, where we want to control everything. Only when there is a situation where we can open our hands to other possibilities will the root of love reveal itself.

....

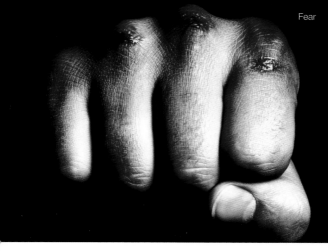

Now, referring back to the last section on Relationship you can probably see if you are living in a relationship with yourself that is tied up with love or fear. I have found in my work over the years that all our reactions originate from the basis of our own relationship with ourselves. Even in my own life I am constantly reminded that my insecurities sometimes come to the surface and run amok, and the fear is then lived out. It is sometimes hard to choose a different strategy, but we refuse to at our own peril.

If unconditional love casts out all fear then surely we just have to love ourselves? 'I can't possibly do that.' I hear you cry. Well that's the whole point of the next section. So much of our culture tells us that we must not love ourselves, as this is just too arrogant, so you will be pleased to know that there is another way – one that is calm, peaceful and humble.

If we look back at the path we have travelled along to date and see how much fear has been involved, we will be astounded. And the thing is we often justify it to ourselves – deluding ourselves once again.

Someone once asked me during a coaching session, 'Well, everybody lives like this don't they?' My answer was yes, but do we necessarily want to, especially if there is a benefit in choosing another way?

One easy way to experience love for yourself is to just smile. Go on smile now. Feels good doesn't it? Now all you have to do is learn to smile at yourself in a real way. Then share your smile with everyone you meet, too. This will have amazing effects, but be careful: you don't want to get arrested!

Many of you may be asking, 'So you're asking me to love everyone?' Well, yes I am. Imagine the effect!

3. Compassion

Some of you may have found the last section difficult for many reasons. As love has been tainted by many of our experiences and so much emphasis is placed on it, it can sometimes become a difficult word to get to grips with.

Compassion, on the other hand, immediately creates a gentle, peaceful and caring environment. What does compassion mean to you? For some it may convey a feeling of weakness, yet if we break the word down we have 'com', which is a prefix from the Latin preposition cum, signifying: with, together, in conjunction. Now think of the word 'passion' – where does this take you?

For most of us this is a very positive word that evokes a good feeling. Passion contains the elements of love, excitement and fun. If you now add in the 'with, together, in conjunction' when you are dealing with other people, as well as yourself, then the power of that word has increased significantly.

Compassion does not mean that you should feel sorry for yourself, or others, but rather that you should care passionately with them.

It is very important that you take on board a full under-standing of this word, as it is essential in transforming not only your life but also the lives of everyone you come into contact with.

By now you will not be surprised to hear me say that the first person you need to have compassion for is yourself. You need to be able to have compassion for your past. This is extremely important to your whole life. In having compassion for your past you will be able to deal with it in a new way rather than running away from it.

It is also important to have compassion for those people you find difficult to get on with or who are aggressive towards you, as they are only behaving in the way they know how to based on their past experiences and the choices they have made at a certain time.

4. Being able to see

At times we find ourselves in a situation where we can't see the wood for the trees. Not only might this be frustrating for those around us but it can also be very damaging to us. We may know what we are seeing, either consciously or unconsciously, and our brains will protect us from having to deal with any pain and/or change.

There is often an internal dialogue that happens in our subconscious where one part of our mind clearly sees that a particular situation is happening (reality) and the other part thinks it recognises a familiar pattern that we must be protected from experiencing. So the mind stops us from facing the reality because it wants to protect us. As a result, the unhealthy belief is kept alive.

You may know other people who behave in this way (it is often easier to see a particular behaviour in others rather than ourselves). They construct a reality within which to live. They will also sometimes lie to enforce their view of reality and will often appear nervous. Here's an example: when listening to someone recount a story of an event that you have also experienced you might hear them embellish or omit certain facts to create the story that they want. They might say, 'We just said hi', although the reality you saw was that they were locked in intense conversation that no one could break into.

Usually it is because people are living their lives at such a great speed that it prevents them from being able to see, but the thought of slowing down is too scary for them to contemplate. If they allow themselves to be conscious of their behaviour in any way they will experience the fear that it holds for them. The only way we can look carefully at ourselves and reality is to find the courage to face that fear. If we are given any space in which to relax we will simply ignore reality, believing that it is no longer necessary to face up to, and the cycle will repeat itself once again. In these moments we will seek out people who agree with our way of thinking, either through ignorance or because they can no longer be bothered with having to deal with us in a real way, as all their previous attempts have been futile.

It is therefore a brave step for us to take, and it is good to walk that path with trusted friends who will be honest with you. This is a vital step to see reality and will be an indication of where this learned pattern of behaviour has come from.

This process is almost like being in a valley and attempting to see where you are going. It is often better to climb the nearest hill so that you can look at the whole area and see the lie of the land. Here you can take time to sit and look all around you so that you have a much clearer picture of where to go and how to get there. From here you will also be able to see how far away from the path you really are.

5. Dependence and independence

When we are born we are at our most vulnerable and we are totally dependent on others, usually our mother, to feed us and look after us. The psychology of the child still assumes that they are the same person as their mother up until the age of about three to six months. Then they start to become aware of others and the hunt for independence begins. This is quite an amusing battle, as the baby wants to take these steps and yet they are still very dependent upon others.

Events happen and our child brain attempts to make sense of what is going on and will go to extraordinary lengths to protect us from any pain at any level. Therefore, this creates the sense that we are not only correct but it also gives us a sense of who we are. At this point the feeling of independence can be built up further or can sometimes be eroded and then we actually become more dependent on others. It all depends on the individual situations and people involved whether we will become more or less dependent as we grow.

Whatever the outcome, there will be elements of dependence and independence that will lead to stresses being brought into any later relationships that we may have.

Good relationships

Before we look at these stresses it is worthwhile looking at what makes a good relationship, this will highlight the differences found in other relationships that are dependent or independent. For any relationship to work effectively and healthily, it must be neither dependent nor independent, as this would cause the relationship to be out of balance. Therefore, a new territory needs to be created where each party is interdependent. This means that although you are an individual in your own right, you are working for a greater result: a relationship that can grow to be rewarding and strong. As Stephen Covey simply puts it, in his book *The 7 Habits of Highly Effective People*, 'The result is greater than the sum of all the parts.'[5]

Coming from a sporting background it is easy for me to use the following analogy. Imagine a two-person cycling team. The object of the team is to get the best overall result for each of the individuals and the team itself. Obviously, if you are a very good cyclist you would want a cyclist of a similar standard to be in your team. At times one of you will lead and the other one of you will tuck in behind and sit in the slipstream to conserve energy. Another time one of you will have to give encouragement to the other, especially for the tough hill climbs. Shouting and screaming may not be the best way to do this!

At other times it may be beneficial to let one of you race on ahead, especially if that person is stronger at sprinting.

Communication is key, so that both members of the team are totally aware of the overall objective.

In this way the best result is achieved, both members of the team are singing from the same song sheet and are totally happy with the process and the outcome.

Now, let's look at the effect of being dependent and independent within this type of relationship. If one of the cyclists is dependent upon the other one to encourage them constantly then this may have a negative overall effect on the other cyclist and the team result. This can be very draining and is unlikely to produce the best result, as their energies are not being used to focus on the overall goal. A relationship like this, on an ongoing basis, will be a gradual downward spiral.

The best thing to do in this situation would be to sit both parties down and deal with the reality of what is going on and the effects of what would happen if this pattern of behaviour did not change.

If, however, one of the cyclists is independent then they will be thinking only of themselves and will never ask or rely on the other cyclist, or even think about their welfare. You would then have, in effect, two separate cyclists and the combined effect would not be realised.

Any move towards either dependence or independence will tip the balance and make the relationship a great deal harder. So in being an Exceptional Person you will have to look at being interdependent at all times when in a relationship with other people. One way of demonstrating this is as follows:

Independent   Interdependent   Dependent

6. Trust

Imagine on your journey along 'the road less travelled' there is a rope bridge that you have to cross. You know the one – the one found only in an Indiana Jones movie. Your guidebook tells you that it is safe to cross. Your mind leaps into survival mode: are you sure that you can trust the guidebook, and, more importantly, the bridge? Then you will wonder whether you can trust your own mind and its many questions.

There may be others around you who you know very well, and they tell you that the bridge is safe. However, somewhere in your memory you are reminded of the time when you trusted them and they let you down. Then along comes a stranger who also tells you that the bridge is safe to cross and, although you still have a little fear, you step out.

Hold on. So let's get this straight. Everyone around you tells you that the bridge is safe to cross and so does the guidebook; and then along comes some stranger – AND YOU BELIEVE THEM!

This just goes to highlight how childlike our minds can be. As we have no previous memory of this new person there is no reference on which to base an argument of no trust and we trust them.

However, another scenario might be where we take a range of information from many different sources and put it all together in our own way so that we have only to trust

ourselves. To our friend or a stranger this might appear that we do not value their opinion or trust them.

Again, we might give out these signals consciously or unconsciously. Either way, we will receive less trust in return.

As we will discuss later, by being transparent (in other words being open in all areas of your life) you will break down the divisions that are present in your life and you will become easier to trust because less information will have been hidden from certain areas of your life.

It is very easy for us to distrust people, especially when we have asked them, or expected them, to do something and they have let us down. We become the champion of the cause never to trust them again. However, let's look at the other principles that we have discussed already to see what our position in this whole process is.

Usually when we ask someone to do something this request passes through a filter in their mind that introduces their own beliefs and meaning to it. They may have not taken the time to understand the reason behind you making the request and, therefore, not put it on their importance list. Also, have you made the request in the way that they can understand it?

As we discussed earlier, in order to trust, you have to start the process from a root of unconditional love. If it is uncon-ditional then there is no expectation.

The building blocks

The first building block is communication. This has to be effective on every level. The next building block is honesty. With both communication and honesty working in a two-way manner trust is born. If you introduce a blemish into love, communication and/or honesty, trust will also be tarnished. However, a note of caution should be raised at this point:

CAUTION: not everyone will be working in the same way as you.

As discussed earlier, this is because people will have formed a view of who we are and will want us to conform to it – people generally dislike change.

This is not an excuse to trust, or distrust, everyone but rather to treat them with unconditional love and work out where they are coming from. You will have the ability to do this although there may be something that blocks you from wanting to see it. If the other person's intentions are dishonourable you will be able to tell (although there may be something within you that quite enjoys their actions, as it fulfils a need within you).

Are you seeing how this jigsaw puzzle is assembling? In developing the relationship with ourselves, are we being honest with ourselves? If we are not then the likelihood is that we do not even trust ourselves, and guess what we will end up portraying? That's right – no trust.

And, yes, keep going: where may this lack of trust come from? Go all the way back to the beginning of the book and ask yourself, 'What is it that I do not want to have to deal with from my past?' Do you see now?

Trust is a key element in how we develop relationships. If we do not fully trust ourselves and others, people will experience only a percentage of the real us. When trust is betrayed at an early age by someone we are taught to trust, a real chasm will be created. The mind creates a situation whereby it both trusts and distrusts the person at the same time. With every relationship that is created from this point onwards there will be elements of trust and distrust, as this is what the mind needs to confirm its own definition. The thought process behind it is that you have reached this far in life safely, so by keeping the pattern the same you will be OK.

Yet how can any relationship based on this truly flourish? The sad news is that it cannot in a healthy way. People unaware of this pattern of trust and distrust will begin to alienate others towards them, as other people tend not to want to be around those who do not trust them, unless it fulfils a need that they have. Those people may, on the other hand, not be prepared to be honest with the distrusting person so he or she will not know what others really think of them.

7. Transparency

Earlier we looked at the benefits of being in an interdependent relationship so that you will achieve good results when working with others, and that the only way you can achieve this is to be in control of your feelings and emotions.

One of the ways that you can achieve this is to be totally transparent in your life. This is different from being open. Being open is usually about one area of your life, whereas transparency is openness across all areas of your life. Why should this be so important?

Compartmentalising our lives into the different constituents of work, social and family, and the compartments that we further create within these areas, requires energy. It requires energy not only to create the walls between the compartments but it also requires energy to safeguard information from travelling from one compartment to another.

By this I am not suggesting that you tell everyone everything

– this could have disastrous effects for many reasons – just be transparent at the appropriate level. By doing this you will find that your life will run much more smoothly. To demonstrate this principle, consider the following:

Imagine your life as a perfect sphere travelling along a perfectly smooth surface. It takes little effort to roll along and you travel in your intended direction. Now imagine a spike protruding from the sphere. This will alter its path because the spike will either make contact with the surface or the weight of the spike will pull the sphere in a different direction. Imagine if you now add a further five spikes. Initially the sphere will move as normal if given enough impetus at the start, and then its movement will become erratic and the sphere will eventually arrive at a standstill in a much shorter time.

The only way for the sphere to run smoothly again is to push the spikes into the sphere or remove them altogether and it can, once again, carry on as before.

Although this is a simple analogy you can see my point that compartmentalising our lives requires a great deal more energy and we would benefit from becoming more transparent. Be also aware that the spikes are already within us and it is our choice as to whether or not we deploy them.

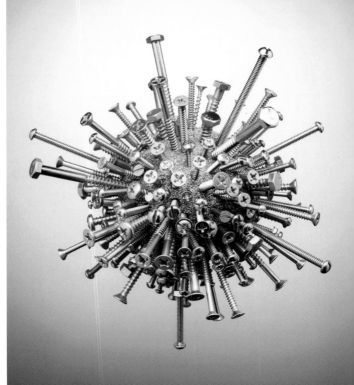

Being relaxed

Imagine how much more relaxed you would be if your life was fully transparent? 'Relaxed?' I hear you cry! 'You must be joking – this would cause even more stress!' If this is the case then look at the motives behind this thought. One of the possible reasons for not wanting transparency in your life is born out of a fear of being exposed or found out. If, however, you are behaving in a way that is full of integrity and respectful of others (interdependent) then you will have nothing to fear.

This may be quite an uncomfortable realisation for some as you may be very aware that you are not behaving with integrity. If this is true you will also be coming up with many reasons as to why this is the case and that there is nothing you can do differently. Well, you can if you want to. By doing it differently you will not only be letting go of stress within you but you will also be giving others more of the real you – a gift.

8. Meekness

Although meek may have connotations of weakness and suffering, I prefer to use it in the terms of how it was once described to me:

Meekness is as follows: imagine a wild horse that is running along with reins flailing. It is an extremely powerful animal that has huge potential as a racing or working horse. However, it needs to know how to be handled so that its strength and full capabilities can be harnessed. At the moment there is a great deal of wasted energy and ineffectiveness. It will take time for it to learn how to use all of its strengths so that it can be effective in all situations. The untamed horse is noisy and runs here and there without purpose and direction. The tamed thoroughbred horse, however, has strength and humility, love and compassion for all, and is non-threatening and not intimidating. Everyone can sense that this is an amazing animal with hidden strength.

In a nutshell: harnessed strength! Imagine how this would manifest itself within you: it would be humble, gentle and yet silently strong and powerful. Nobody could fail to notice this, even if they did not particularly like the look of it.

9. Control

While we strive to achieve our desired end result our mind can go into overtime, devising schemes and plans to ensure that others conform to the pattern that we believe will give us the outcome that we seek. When we arrive at this desired outcome, there is a feeling of, 'Yes – mission accomplished!' The road behind us might resemble a picture of destruction, but, nevertheless, as far as we are concerned we have succeeded. This, then, is the world of control and domination.

We tell ourselves that the more control we can take of a given situation the greater the chance we will have of achieving the result that we want. Our childlike minds are at work here. What we often don't realise, or we ignore, however, is that on some level everyone else will be thinking this, too, so a power struggle will be brewing.

If we actually allow everyone to have his or her own input we may accomplish a far more advantageous result, way beyond what we thought possible. As an Exceptional Person you may have to take the lead in a given situation to get the ball rolling and encourage everyone to work together.

The beginnings of control

First, let us just review where control comes from. Is control born out of love or fear? If freedom originates from love, then control (the clenched fist) originates from fear. But what is it a fear of? Usually it is fear of the unknown, and it can be dressed up in many different guises. Your mind may take you to a place diametrically opposite to your desired outcome where no alternative will exist, making you believe that control is the only solution. Fear will stop you from exploring possible alternatives. You might also be worried that if you don't achieve your desired outcome you will have a sense of failure, non-acceptance and rejection. These fears are childlike beliefs.

Exercise

Take a moment to consider a situation that is relevant in your life now. Look at how controlling you are being. Think about all of the possible positive outcomes that could be set in motion by reducing some of your control. Imagine how others are being impaired by your control and what the benefits might be if you reduced it in some way.

Now I hear you say, 'Well, there is no way that I am letting go of any of my control to those idiots!' You may have a point to some degree. So rather than keeping them as idiots look at the way in which you can develop their skills to manage themselves if they were to be given the freedom and responsibility to do something.

Within the work context, if you know that each time you give someone a task they are going to fail, then STOP and look at your part within that process to see how you can secure a win-win solution.

Each time you feel control is taking over, look at the role your fear is playing and look for the flip side so that there can be a healthier and better outcome.

III

Alchemy

Alchemy

So, by now you have assessed the lie of the land and looked at the many facets that make up the Human Being. By drawing together Parts I and II the Exceptional Person is beginning to grow. It is unlikely that you will have been living your life like this to date (well done, though, if you have) and the next part of growing as an Exceptional Person will be to live it out. Therefore, in order to do this and create alchemy there are a few additional factors to think about. In some cases they can make a huge difference between knowing what makes the Exceptional Person and being that person; think about this: knowing without being is not knowing at all.

1. Support and surroundings

Imagine that as you were growing up you were surrounded by people who continually supported you in whatever you did and were there to help you answer all kinds of questions and thoughts that you had. They were there to encourage you in whatever way you needed so that you could explore your dreams and you would learn about life and its many mysteries and treasures. They taught you about an unconditional love that shaped everything that you ever did and people also knew the amazing gift that was within you. Just imagine …

Now think of the flip side of that coin; one where you

received no support and where you were surrounded by people who continually put you down and discouraged you from doing anything.

If this second pattern is learned at an early age the chances are that you would be a relatively negative person, whereas a person from the first situation would be positive most of the time.

Take time to look at the people and physical environment that surround you. Are these people healthy for you? Are they constantly on the take and draining you of your finite source of energy?

Some of these draining people may have been in your life for many years, during which time they have become ever more draining. You don't really enjoy spending time with them but you feel that you should because you can't just cut them out of your life. OK, well have a go at the following:

....

Exercise

Take a blank piece of paper and write ME in the middle. Now draw a small circle around it, then, around the word ME, write the names of the people who are in your life.

Now go round and write either a plus (+) or a minus (–) next to each name depending on whether you think that person has a positive or a negative effect on your life.

....

How does your life look? Imagine if everyone on that piece of paper was a positive. How different would you feel, and how much less stress would you have in your life? It's worth trying to see if you can do anything to bring this change about.

As you will now be aware, the only thing that you can control is you. Go back and look again at being the love that you seek. By being this new person you will attract a new set of people into your life. Also by accepting others as they are, along with their views, you may actually initiate a change in them. You also have to create your boundaries and know where their limits are. You do not need to spend time telling and showing others where those boundaries are; you do, however, need to know what to do when someone encroaches on them.

Some of your friends may not enjoy seeing you take more control of your life and becoming happier, and they may try to disrupt this change with more negative comments. Expect this – it does happen!

You have a choice: see where you are allowing these negative inputs to come from. They may be fulfilling a need in you somewhere, so BEWARE.

Placing boundaries to protect yourself from negativity and making your life better may cause a little disruption to start with as this will be new for you and for those around you. The benefits in the long run, however, will be worthwhile, as you will have only positive influences in your life. Just imagine.

2. Others

If by reading this book you have attempted to make some changes in your life, you may have come across some added resistance from others that you had not been expecting. Rather than your friends and family supporting some of the changes they may have rebutted such advances and quashed any growth or change. So here is a word of warning: they are like everyone else – they do not necessarily like change either. They have been accustomed to you behaving as you were and not as the new you. This different person is something that they are not used to and they can at times challenge you on your new perspectives. These people may be friends, family or business partners and you will have to decide on your preferred course of action in each situation. The best way, I believe, is to put into practice what you have read. Those people are behaving in the way they know how, so give them some time to get used to you. If, after a while, they still do not like the new you, then you will have to decide whether a true friend is one who does not allow you to change.

Although this may seem a little severe, it is just intended to highlight what you might come up against. Remember, they think they are right in what they are doing and there will be many reasons why they are not happy about things around them changing.

3. Wisdom

You have been introduced to many facets of life throughout this book and you can choose when to employ them. The wisdom surrounding this decision is in your hands. Seek to be wise at all times and remember that the results will be different when you begin with the outstretched palm of freedom – they will be way beyond your wildest dreams. Go on have a go.

Are you prepared to give up everything you know in order to embrace everything that you dare to believe?

4. The future and beyond

So, you have now completed this short handbook. There may be things that you agree with and other things that you don't. Whatever side you find yourself on I would ask you to be at least open to exploring the issues that I have raised. You may find that there is some truth in what I have written.

These are my thoughts on these subjects but in no way should they be taken as gospel. I believe, however, that the book describes the truly Exceptional Person and that peeling away the layers that hide this inner person is indeed worthwhile, not only for the individual concerned but for everyone who comes into contact with them.

You will encounter many things in life and the same situations will repeatedly occur until you learn their lessons. Once you have learned you will find that life will uncover more of what it wants to share with you.

Happy journeys, my friends, and I look forward to meeting many of you Exceptional People along the way.

In the meantime please do feel free to contact me at jc@akindred.com – I look forward to hearing from you.

Jez

References

1. Daniel Goleman, *Destructive Emotions*, Bloomsbury, 2003, pp. 19-21.

2. Georges Philips and Tony Jennings, *My Little Book of Verbal Antidotes*, ICET Ltd, 1999 repr. 2003.

3. Stephen Covey, *The 7 Habits of Highly Effective People*, Franklin Covey, 1990, p. 235.

4. J. Bowlby, *'Maternal care and mental health'*, World Health Organization Monograph, serial no. 2, 1951; and *Attachment and Loss, Vol. 1, Attachment*, Basic Books, 1969.

5. Stephen Covey, *The 7 Habits of Highly Effective People*, Franklin Covey, 1990, p. 163.

Thanks

To the people in my past – thank you for all the experiences and for what I have learnt so far,

To the people in my life today – thank you for all your continuing love, friendship and support,

And to the people in my future – thank you in advance for what I have yet to experience and learn.

Special thanks to Daniel Goleman and Georges Philips for granting permission to reproduce extracts from their respective books.

A big thank you to all who have helped in contributing to this book and a special thank you to my editor Jan Cutler and my designer James Cartledge for their patience and expertise.

Notes